ARO

CHOICE

MAN'S MOST IMPORTANT POWER

ironPEN

CHOICE: MAN'S MOST IMPORTANT POWER

ISBN: 978-978-971-880-1

Published in The Federal Republic of Nigeria by:
IRON PEN KALMA KRAFT LTD
Mr. Simon Ndacks' Residence, Opposite Power House Office,
Akwanga, Nasarawa State.
ironpenpublishing@gmail.com
info@ironpenbooks.net
www.ironpenbooks.net
08033569841

Unless otherwise indicated, all Scripture quotations are taken from the New King James Version of the Bible (NKJV). Scripture quotations marked NIV and AMP are taken from the New International Version and The Amplified Bible respectively.

CONTENTS

INTRODUCTION

Heaven is God's throne but the earth He has handed over to man. Though He controls the heavens and likewise rules over the affairs of men, it is very instructive to note that God does not in the practical sense of it rule over the affairs of all men. He only rules over the affairs of the men that choose to relate with Him as Lord. He is not a tyrant. God's unmatchable, illimitable and incalculable omnipotent power becomes restricted when it comes to human affairs. Why? Because He gave man the power even He Himself would not tamper with: the power of choice. That's why He created man not as a zombie or automaton, fully programmed to obey Him, but as a free moral agent with the great power to choose what the outcome of His days on earth and even in the afterlife will be. It is for this reason the author makes bold to assert in this book that the greatest power in heaven is the power of God, while THE MOST IMPORTANT POWER ON EARTH IS MAN'S POWER OF CHOICE.

I don't believe in the overwhelming complexity of luck and the omnipotence of chance – the two foundation stones of the *"what will be, will be"* philosophy – which I believe is not scriptural in the least. I believe in choice and consequence. And for what it's worth, luck and chance only happen to people who have decided to abandon their power of choice in the state of perennial inertia. With our God-given power to choose, we become responsible for whatever becomes of our lives - good or bad.

I understand that the term *force majeure* which literally means 'superior force' comes in handy in legal parlance to describe circumstances that are beyond man's control. These are sometimes called the acts of God which usually hit man like stray bullets; completely unforeseen and uncalculated but whose effects are most devastating. For instance, the slew of woes that befell Job was not a product of his choice. The woes were permitted by God's sovereignty; they were okayed by the Great Monarch of Heaven from a position that was way beyond the scope of Job's power of choice. However, when Job got in the picture, he still had a choice to make: curse God and die or hang on to God's faithfulness in the midst of his darkest, most excruciating hour. You see, no matter how bad or hopeless it is, we always have a choice to make. One of the greatest lies floating around is 'I have no choice!'

Those who have a functional relationship with God don't recklessly wait for the highly improbable waves of fate (produced by luck and chance) to help them surf on life's high sea, they deliberately engage the living God by walking according to His precepts and statutes to shower His favour upon them. Life is not a game of luck and/or chance my friend; it's a game of choice.

Right and wrong, good and bad, life and death shall always remain before us. The onus is always on us to choose which would eventually become our lot. Every human being – saved and unsaved alike, stands on the cross roads of life; that critical moment in which they have to trudge through the fork in the road and make the choice that would influence the entire course of their life. In some cases, it's usually an uneasy, adrenaline-stormed moment in which the content of one's character is put to the test.

CHOICE

Those who sit on the fence will surely be commandeered by the recalcitrance of luck and chance and become victims of life's offence. Those who dilly dally trail; while those who choose, always impactfully hit the hammer to the nail. Indecision is a malady much deadlier than the most deadly disease under heaven - for while a natural disease kills the body, indecision kills the will. A man with an impotent will can produce nothing in the world's field.

This book has been written to help spur you not just to learn to make a choice – but to make the right choices every day of your life. That's the assignment that the Great Monarch of Zion has given the author: to get you to that place of endless victory where you are constantly inspired to make the right choices. All right choices point to God and His cause.

May He who has the power to make and mar, make you as you journey through the pages of this book. May the eyes of your understanding be enlightened as you get motivated and educated by the Holy Spirit about which way your life should go. May you brook no indecision in your journey of faith.

The contents of this book are synthesized directly from the wealth of Arome Osayi's spoken ministry. I enjoin you by the mercies of God to prayerfully consider the matters treated here in. All will be well when you and I choose well.

Rabeeu Nas Madaki
March, 2019
AKWANGA, NIGERIA

ACKNOWLEDGMENTS

It is a great honour to publish the word God has given to me for my generation. The Lord has blessed me with an incredible team that is yoked with me in gospel of the kingdom of our Lord Jesus Christ. With them, the yoke has been easy and the burden light. With the right team, it does not get cosier but sure gets better. I cannot mention everyone by name for the obvious want of space; but my gratitude is shoreless!

I thank my darling wife for the great support and sacrifice; for making the home front completely impenetrable to the machinations of hell and a centre of kingdom operation. Her partnership is central to all the strides we have made so far to the glory of God Most High. I thank my children, Joshua and Esther, for magnanimously adjusting to daddy's endless trips for the sake of the kingdom.

I thank my father in faith, Dr. John E. Akpami, for his depth of wisdom, precious oversight and fatherly companionship. I never cease to thank God for bringing me to your fold, daddy. The Lord Himself is your reward.

I thank my dear friend and covenant brother, Gideon Odoma, for taking time out of his very busy schedule to go through the manuscript in order to tighten every loose end. Your labour of love can only be rewarded by the Great One.

I thank the publishing team at Iron Pen Kalma Kraft Ltd for developing the manuscripts and coordinating the production of this book. You guys have been an immense blessing.

I thank my Remnant Christian Family for giving their all to ensure the mandate to *strive for the rebirth of apostolic Christianity* is now a global phenomenon. I am most honoured to have you guys.

Glory be to the Shepherd of our souls!

Dedication

This book is dedicated to the faithfulness of God, which is a resource that is more reliable than silver and gold!

CHAPTER ONE

IN THE BEGINNING THERE WAS CHOICE

'And out of the ground the Lord God made every tree to grow that is pleasant to the sight and good for food. The tree of life was also in the midst of the garden, and the tree of the knowledge of good and evil....... And the Lord God commanded man, saying, "of every tree of the garden you may freely eat, but of the tree of the knowledge of good and evil you shall not eat, for in the day that you eat of it you shall surely die'

—Genesis 2:9,16-17, NKJV

Man, the crown of God's creation was created to take charge of all that God created under heaven. He was designed and thoroughly equipped by God to manage every created thing on earth. He was charged by God to dominate and subdue the earth by creatively multiplying and fruitfully expanding his seed to fill up the earth. This great assignment was to begin from a place called the Garden of Eden - which was to serve as man's administrative headquarters. It was from there he would administer the whole earth. It was an enviable height of honour God placed him upon. It was such a magnificent honour that would make the psalmist harp the following words:

CHOICE

'When I view and consider your heavens,
The work of your fingers, the moon and the stars,
Which you have ordained and established,
What is man that you are mindful of him,
and the son of (earthborn) man that you care for him?
Yet you have made him but a little lower than God (or heavenly beings),
and you have crowned him with glory and honor.
You made him to have dominion over the works of your hands;
You have put all things under his feet'

—Psalm 8:3-6, Amp

The Psalmist captures it all, in great wonder and deep reflection of how man – such small and seemingly feeble being would be saddled with the responsibility of governing the whole earth. Well, God decided it so.

The earth was man's bulk assignment but the Garden of Eden would be his primary place of assignment – the epicentre of his work on earth. He was supposed to both care for and defend it. And according to Genesis chapter two (our Scripture of consideration above), there were available to man three categories of trees in the Garden of Eden:

1. Every tree pleasant to the sight and good for food
2. The tree of life
3. The tree of knowledge of good and evil.

Now these three categories of trees were all edible to man. The first category was meant to meet man's aesthetic and nutritional needs, hence, the terms 'pleasant to the sight' and 'good for food'. This category of trees was designed and framed to cater to man's every dietary need. Man was free to partake of every tree species that fell into this category.

The second category of trees was the tree of life which the Bible says was in the centre of the Garden. Scripture is deliberately silent about God's instruction to man on the consumption of the fruit of this tree for one obvious reason: that man would have to choose whether or not to eat from it. God neither forbade nor encouraged him to eat of the tree of life though eating it would make man immortal on earth. So that man could fully become God's extension on earth. That as God is eternal and immortal in the heavens, not aging or fainting, so would man be on earth.

The third category of trees was the tree of the knowledge of good and evil which I would like to call the tree of death for the purpose of our study. This tree was found in the same perimeter as the tree of life – in the centre of the Garden which we have said was the epicentre of man's work on earth. If you ask me, I would say the trees of life and of the knowledge of good and evil or the tree death stood side by side in the middle of the Garden beckoning on man, day and night. Quietly and tirelessly they sent signals across to man to engage his power to vicariously choose what the destiny of humanity would be. This is very interesting because it would be the first time God would place this much power in the hand of any one of His creatures. There was no other creature in heaven and on earth that had the power to vicariously decide the destiny of their kind. Only man was given such power.

It is worthy of note that the power of choice is not peculiar to man. In heaven, the angelic hosts also have the power to choose. They are only allowed, however, to exercise such power in deferential consonance and solemn synchronisation with the authority of Heaven's Great Monarch - God Almighty. Any exercise of such power that violates God's eternally constituted authority is crushed by the full weight of God's power (2 Peter 2:4). The exercise of the power of choice against the eternally constituted authority and will of God is called transgression.

For instance, when Lucifer sinned by choosing to rebel against God, his sin did not besmirch the entire heavenly hosts. Only those angels who chose to partake in his sin were cast out of heaven along with him. So, there is in effect none other of God's creatures, be it in heaven or on earth that could choose for their kind. This is what made the power God gave man to choose in the Garden unprecedented. For this power was so vicarious that man could decide the destiny of the whole human race which at the time was cocooned in his loins.

Why would God give one man – Adam – such a humongous doze of power to decide the destiny of his kind? It's called faith my friend. Long before it would be required for man to place his unalloyed, unreserved faith in God, God did that first, with more at stake. This is because God would never ask man to make a commitment that He Himself has not made in gargantuan proportions and against much greater odds. Before God asked man to love Him, He loved man first. Before God would ask man to have faith in Him, He placed His faith in man first, and long before man would be required to choose God, God first elected within the council of the Godhead to choose man to both bear His image and likeness and lead His creation under heaven.

Note that the exercise of man's power of choice was not only going to directly impact and shape the destiny of his kind, it was also going to have multilayered, multidimensional and transgenerational impact across the ranks of all of creation under heaven. Animals, plants, the elements and the very earth itself were going to get hit by the consequence of man's power of choice.

By giving man the extraordinary power to choose, God effectively put in man's hand the power switch that could either light up or darken the whole of creation - all man needed to do was flick it however he chose. You would not blame God for bestowing upon man this much honour - man was choicest creation!

The motif of the Garden of Eden had every tree surrounding the trees of life and death. The arrangement of the Garden was flawless, with the tree that mattered the most standing gallantly and verdantly in the midst of it. Of all the trees in the Garden, God only commanded man not to eat of the tree of death. God fully spelt out the consequences of having anything to do with the tree of death - eternal death, or, eternal separation from Him. Now here is the big picture: man was created to manage the works of God's hands on earth but he had to pass a test to qualify experientially for that task. God placed man in the Garden of Eden to pass the greatest test on which the destiny of the whole human race hung. It was a test whose result would be allinclusive, in that, failing or passing it would affect the seed of man till the end of time. This means that the destiny of mankind depended so much on the outcome of the test.

God's desire was for man to pass this test. That was why He went all the way to give man a success tip by telling him to steer clear from the tree of death. In all fairness, God gave man the tools he needed to pass this test. Because by singling out the tree of death and blackballing it, it seemed as if He was telling man; 'Eat every tree, eat the tree of life and ensure you don't touch the tree of death. If you do this, you and your seed will forever be with me'. God had His self-imposed though and would not do for man what man should do for Himself.

God's awesome power was displayed in His creation of heaven and earth. By creating man, He added colour to the grandeur of

His creative might - more like the perfect crescendo to a masterpiece symphony. In creating man He put within man's earthly frame a power so magnificent but latent, that even He Himself was bound by honour not to violate - the power of choice.

This power is latent and requires the full engagement of the will to be activated. God created man in order not to have a fully programmed robot on earth that understands nothing but executes the commands of his maker in heaven. He wanted a person who would willingly choose to depend on Him. He created man's will so that man would play a lead role in determining the course and outcome of his life by making choices. The power of choice was supposed to help man govern the works of God's hands on earth. Since he is the crown of God's creation and governor of God's creation on earth by design, it would be safe to deduce therefore that the highest power in heaven is God's power and the most important power on earth is man's power of choice.

Life is replete with concatenation of events, circumstances, opportunities and challenges - big or small, rough or smooth, friendly or hostile, planned or unplanned, straight forward or labyrinthine, black or white, grey or colourless - that compel the utilisation of the power of choice on a daily basis. Every living soul under heaven must of a necessity choose whether or not to engage their power of choice on a daily basis. Making no choice is a choice in itself.

This brings us to the big question: what is choice? Choice is all about engaging the will power to pick between or among options that are presented to us throughout life. These options may come in the form of opportunities, possibilities or alternatives, all of which have the innate force to propel and steer the entire course of one's life. Based on this, I would like to introduce to you a tree that was silently present and yet not physically present in the Garden of Eden – I call it The Tree of Choice – whose fruit man had to present to the one whom he chose to be the centre of his life.

The tree of life, if eaten, would forever connect man with God and disconnect man from the devil, making God the centre of man's life. The tree of death, if eaten, would forever disconnect man from God and put him under the thumb of the devil, making corruption and death the centre of man's life. To partake of either tree, man had to first, willingly surrender the fruits of his tree of choice to God or the devil.

As it were, man was faced with two options: Life and death. Having either of them as his lot would be solely determined by the choice he made. There it was, the destiny of mankind hanging on the choice of the first couple on earth – Adam and Eve.

The story of the human race took a dismal turn when Adam and Eve chose death over life by surrendering their tree of choice to the devil and eating of the tree of death. Yes, the devil came around and did flash the most appealing stratagem at man, but the most he did was to suggest – present an antithetical alternative to God's word. Had they heeded God's warning and obeyed His command, the devil's glib talk would have counted for nothing. But by stretching forth their hands in disobedience and reaching for the forbidden fruit of the tree of death, their whole life and that of the endless generations that would spring from them would be thrown into the devil's dungeon and cauldron. Oh no, man fell from the height of glory God had placed him. His rebellion against God engendered creation's rebellion against him and his descendants. The woes that befell him became more and more convoluted. Today, after multiplied thousands of years of human history, the earth still aches from the aftermath of the choice Adam and Eve made. There is not enough space in this book to outline them for they are beyond counting.

Spikes of disappointment pierced through God's heart. There was unrest in heaven. God's plan for man was seemingly hanging on a precarious balance. Something must be done and fast. Man had chosen death over life. There was nothing God and the hosts of heaven could do. Man had chosen his own fate, filled-in doom into the blank page given him in the Garden wherein to write his destiny and that of his offspring. The whole situation was a lamentable one – the obituary of *mankind.*

The elements which once interplayed to sing songs of beauty and honour and freshness suddenly turned pale with corruption and began to yell inglorious requiems for the destiny of man; the stench of which choked sweetness and balance out of creation. This gave rise to chaotic disorder among the different ranks and species of creation under heaven.

As a swift counter measure, God had to prevent man from further stretching forth his hand to eat of the tree of life. Eating of the tree of life would make him immortal and eternal like God. But eating of the tree of life in his fallen state would spell unquenchable doom as it would make him immortally and eternally irredeemable – just like the fallen angels. To redeem him, God had to drive him out of the Garden until the fullness of time in which His redemption package would be ready in Jesus Christ. The story of man in the Garden of Eden ends tragically thus:

> *Then the Lord God said, 'Behold, the man has become like one of Us, to know good and evil. And now, lest he put out his hand and take also of the tree of life, and eat, and live*

forever"–therefore the Lord sent him out of the Garden of Eden to till the ground. From which he was taken. So He drove out the man, and He placed Cherubim at the east of the Garden of Eden, and a flaming sword which turned every way, to guard the way to the tree of life.'

—Genesis 3:22-24

I could almost hear God say; "Man has made his choice. There is very little we can do. Let him bear the consequences of his choice until the time is right for his redemption.' God made the tree of life inaccessible for many generations until His only begotten Son was conceived and born by a virgin. Thank God Jesus came to reset, restore and redeem mankind by obediently allowing God to birth the new creation through Him!

To bring this home, I would like to say that a whole generation is determined by the strength of your choice! The power of choice bestowed on you and I by God is by design vicarious in nature and consequence. This means the choices we make do not only affect us, they also affect the generations cocooned in our loins directly or tangentially – those we are privileged by God to influence. I can especially attest to this simple but timeless and universal truth: choice is man's most important power under heaven

Many of the promotions, advancements, growth and development I have enjoyed in my personal life and ministry have been underpinned by the choices I have made. Some of the choices were extremely difficult and disrupted my whole personal arrangements of comfort. Some of the most painful disappointments, heartaches and discouragements I have experienced have also been borne on the back of choices I have made. The obedience of Christ has remained my compass as I navigate the world's wild – on this journey of faith.

CHOICE

Bitter or sweet, I have learned to always synchronize my choices with God's flawless will – for therein lies the key to unlocking the blessings of heaven over my life and the lives of those who listen to God's word committed to me for my generation. I know by study, instruction and experience that the choices I make do not only affect me but also affect those who are connected to me. This is why over the years, I have made it a point of solemn goal to exercise my God-given power of choice circumspectly and in total deference to Jesus Christ!

The seriousness of choice is defined by the truth that we become a part of God's family by the new birth (salvation) but become partakers of the kingdom of heaven by choice! Not everyone who is a part of God's family is an active partaker of the kingdom of heaven. This is because to be an active partaker of the kingdom of heaven, one must deliberately engage their power of choice to submit to the lordship of Jesus Christ who bears the government of God. This I have dealt with extensively in both volumes of my book Kingdom Recalibration.

CHAPTER TWO

THE ETERNAL AND RELATIONAL GOD

Then the Lord God called to Adam and said to him, "Where are you?" So he said, "I heard Your voice in the garden, and I was afraid because I was naked; and I hid myself." And He said, "Who told you that you were naked? Have you eaten from the tree of which I commanded you that you should not eat?"

—Genesis 3:9-11, NKJV

The eternality of God forever remains a mystery no human mind can fathom. The simple but solemn fact that God's uncreated infiniteness cannot be defined by finite parameters constantly eludes those who try. 'Forever' is His domain and time is just a tool in His hand. Eternity itself cannot unravel Him. By the farthest stretch of the imagination and the deepest plunge of contemplation, the nature and character of God cannot be significantly understood within the context of created finiteness. To get a grasp of who God is in terms of His character and nature requires an express revelation from Him through His Spirit.

It takes faith to believe that He exists in the first place. Rationalizing and analyzing Him, His possible origin, how He came about His power, and so on (these are finite parameters);

only leaves the human mind in the thick maze of confusion and incorrigibly mangles the sanity of the heart.

God's eternality is so inscrutable that any attempt to use human tools to search it out leads to wild confusion. The depth of His wisdom is bottomless. The source of His life and power cannot be touched by the most extensive and expansive human attempt. That's why the two extremes the human heart can ply are: faith and foolishness. It takes faith to believe that He exists even though His existence cannot be touched or felt by the five senses. It takes foolishness to dismiss His existence simply because it does not lend itself to the probing of human wit and whim. The psalmist says,

"The fool has said in his heart, 'there is no God'". (Psalm 53:1)

While the writer of Hebrews says,

> *But without faith it is impossible to please and be satisfactory to Him. For whoever would come near to God must [necessarily] believe that God exists and that He is the rewarder of those who earnestly and diligently seek Him [out].*
>
> **—Hebrews 11:6, AMP**

God as an eternal being is all-knowing, all powerful, all-present, never-dying, never aging, never fading, all-wise, etc. He is all in all. He was never born and does not have a beginning. He does not have an end. Yet the beginning and end of all things subsist in Him. These attributes are what make Him divine. No technological, scientific and philosophical tool can calculate the size of His divinity. Someone once said trying to fathom Him is like trying to empty an ocean with a table spoon!

The angels in heaven forever marvel at His ever-unfolding power, wisdom and glory. He is inexhaustible! His eternality makes Him know all there was, there is and there will be; makes Him do things that are humanly impossible and makes Him have His presence throughout the vast stretch of time, space and eternity. In a sense, everything in time has already taken place in Him. Yet He is not bored to watch men and women repeat it all through endless ages.

This same eternal God has another side which is totally disparate from His eternality - I call this aspect of Him the relational side. Hence, the term *relational God*. This is the side He takes on in order to have an intimate relationship with humans on whom He has bestowed the magnificent power of choice. God created man primarily to have relationship with Him. Man's assignment was supposed to be an overflow effect from his relationship with God. That's why God came by the Garden in the cool of every day to fellowship with man - a privilege which only man enjoyed in the entire creation. He came to the Garden to commune with man not as the eternal God who knows it all; He came as the relational God - a Being seeking fellowship.

As the eternal God, He knew it all. But as the relational God, He allowed man to use the power He had given Him - the power of choice. That's what made Him enjoy and bask in every moment He spent in fellowship with man and looked forward to the next moment. Knowing it all did not make Him assume on man. He did not say, 'Oh, it is pointless working with man because he'll fall any way'. No, He related with man as a man would with his friend - allowing him make choices that will affect the course of his life. He gave man the fair chance to choose his destiny.

Consequent upon this fact, I would like to state further that there is no person on earth destined for heaven or hell, poverty or riches, fortune or misfortune etc. God allows every man and woman to make their choice at every given point in their life. So when God predestines for man, He neither does so lightly nor presumptuously – He actually writes the script (called destiny) and allows man to choose to either or not act according to the script. It must be noted however, that should man choose to act the script of destiny, God must be the director! God does not despotically make any man or woman to act according to His script. No leashes, no fetters ...just man's free will.

The ultimate manifestation and crystallization of the relational side of God is Jesus Christ whom the Bible say

> *Who, although being essentially one with God and in the form of God [possessing the fullness of the attributes which make God God]... But stripped Himself [of all privileges and rightful dignity], so as to assume the guise of a servant (slave), in that He became like men and was born a human being.*
>
> **—Philippians 2:6, 7, AMP**

You see, Jesus was and still is fully God and fully man – with the right amount of balance between His divinity and humanity. His humanity (with its attendant limitations) cloaked His divinity. This made Him the God-man. As the God-man, He had to learn like an ordinary man. He too, had the power to choose like every other man. As we would later see, the most important moment in Jesus' earthly ministry was when He had to make a choice to either yield to God's will and die for humanity to be redeemed or refuse to yield and preserve Himself for mankind to remain within the clutches of death. He had to vicariously choose between obedience and disobedience, between life and death – more like what the first man did in the Garden of Eden. This singular exercise of His power to choose would determine the destiny of the new creation.

Genesis 3:9-11, reveals the relational side of God. The eternal, all-knowing God seems to be roaming the Garden looking for Adam and Eve. Or, like a man lost in the jungle He screams, 'Adam where are you?' Is this not a question too mortal to be asked by the infinite God? How could the all-knowing God comb through the midst of the Garden looking for the man He created? Was He blind? No, He wasn't - He was just being relational. The bridge that connected Him to Adam was destroyed.

In His being relational He would not get past Adam's choices, and would not equally violate them. The bridge that linked them to Him in this wonderful romance was their choice of obedience. As soon as they disobeyed, they seemed to have vanished from His radar. That's why He had to go through the hassle of enquiring of their whereabouts. On this plane of existence, He decided He would only – as it were – know by asking. That's why He rained a barrage of questions an Adam. Curiosity can be sensed as He quizzed,

'Who told you that you were naked?' He asks Adam bluntly. No reply.

So He probes further.

'Have you eaten from the tree I commanded you that you should not eat? Come on, talk to me Adam!?

'I heard your voice in the Garden, and I was afraid because I was naked... and I hid myself', Adam replies after managing to dispel fright from his throat.

The voice of God, which flowed sweet to Adam's soul like an age old wine suddenly spooked him. Once upon a memorable time, he was naked and was not ashamed but now he quivers in fright for the same reason, before God. Prior to this time he looked forward to hearing the heart-soothing footsteps of God advance toward him in the Garden for fellowship. But now he hides and runs away from God – going around weaving shrubs into aprons to cover his seemingly embarrassing nakedness.

Man's choice was of phenomenal proportion – everything depended on it. When he made it, the domino effect set in: he drifted and strayed farther and farther from God, he lost his way, instead of depending on God, he began to lean on his limited understanding. This cursed state of existence was what he bequeathed to the whole of mankind. By that one choice he made Adam gave the devil a helping hand in corrupting the template of creation from which his offspring's would rise. The devil's skewed plan for the ultimate corruption of man took instant effect. One choice turned Adam's beautiful beginning to an epic tragedy.

Upon man's failure, God's relational nature did not end. As a matter of fact He remained steadfast and sought more ways to draw man closer to Himself but man's worsening iniquity continued to widen the gap between them – in a sense. God continued to yearn for man's fellowship. As the ages piled upon the stables of history, so did God's nostalgia for befriending and communing with man grow nonstop. But man needed Him even more. And throughout the Old Testament, God sought different avenues to bridge the gap between Himself and humankind. However, it was still going to take man wielding his power of choice to get things straight.

As the eternal God, He knew it all, did it all, but He needed to be more than that to save man. He needed to be more than an Almighty, unapproachable God to man. He needed to be an approachable and relational father who could be touched by man's feelings of infirmities. He was going to present the Tree of

Life once more. Only that this time He would be born in Bethlehem by a virgin, move the earth's surface for thirty-three and a half years, die a vicarious death on a cross for humanity's mammoth sins, bring peace to man's seismic confusion, undo the works and power of the devil and secure eternal victory by making eternal life available and accessible to all. But it would still take man's choice to accept all of this. It would take man's wilful surrendering of his Tree of Choice for God to eat.

CHAPTER THREE

THE HEART OF THE KING IS IN HIS HANDS

The King's heart is in the hand of the Lord, as are the watercourses; He turns it whichever way He wills.

—Proverbs 21:1, AMP

God's kingdom is eternal. His throne is established in eternity with everything in the universe steered according to the counsel of His will. Being the head of the only incorruptible, imperishable kingdom of heaven, every kingdom, crown and throne on earth derives its authority from Him. He is the King of kings.

In kingdom matters, the will of the king is the incontestable frame of reference against which all else is measured. God, being the Supreme King arranges and rearranges all things to fall into alignment with His will. His will is what He wants to do and what He wants to have done.

The hand of God in Scripture connotes His power by which everything is sustained and ruled. By His hand, God pulls down and builds, establishes and destroys, arranges and scatters, and brings everything in conformity with His will. Being the eternal king, His authority extends from heaven to earth and nothing happens without His authorization. The Bible says,

'... His kingdom is an everlasting kingdom, and all dominions shall serve and obey Him'

–Daniel 7: 27c

Now, His mighty hand of power does not only bear everything but also something very curious – the heart of the king. The heart of the king is the seat of decision – it is the centre from where choices are made. A good king has a good heart and an evil king has an evil heart. Someone said a good king listens to the advice of others but follows his heart. God holds the heart of the king and turns it wherever He wishes like courses of rivers.

Why does God turn the heart of the king? This is so that everything will work according to His divine order. It is true God does not interfere with man's choices. But in matters touching on His eternally constituted authority He is every width on earth in the affairs of men either by ruling or overruling. That's why He influences not the choices of ordinary men but kings, yet not breaking the grand rule of allowing men make their decisions by exercising their power of choice.

The difference between a king and an ordinary man is authority. A king has the authority which empowers him to provide oversight for many people under his watch while a common man is primarily responsible for himself. By virtue of authority, a king is not primarily responsible for himself but others. This makes his heart worthy of being held in God's powerful hand. This is one of the many acts of God's sovereignty – which means it cannot be questioned.

God does not interfere with the king's personal choices. He only interferes with those choices of his that touch on his authority – affecting others. Therefore God relates with a king both as a man and then as a man with authority. As a man, the king is allowed to make His choices uninterrupted. As a man with authority, God places His microscope on every choice the king makes and when necessary intervenes. God's heavenly authority is felt on earth through established human authority. All human authority, good or evil, derives validity from God's authority. The heart of every king on earth – righteous or heathen, is in the controlling hand of God.

Throughout the Bible, God never interfered with any king's personal choices. He only got involved directly when His authority was on the verge of being undermined among men, making sure His authority is established on earth among men as it is in heaven. The Bible says concerning kings and rulers on earth who conspired to undermine God's authority thus:

> *The kings of the earth take their places; the rulers take counsel together against the Lord and His Anointed One (the Messiah, the Christ). They say, Let us break their bands [of restraint] asunder and cast their cords [of control] from us. He who sits in the heavens laughs; the Lord has them in derision [and in supreme contempt He mocks them].*
>
> **—Psalms 2:2-4, AMP**

This is a typical example of an authority-based action on earth provoking an authority-based reaction from heaven. When authority is involved, God bypasses protocol, overrules human arrangements underpinned by choices made and decisions taken, leaps across the divide between eternity and time and directly intervenes so as to promptly superimpose the counsel of His will. Let's consider some more examples from Scripture:

> *On an appointed day Herod arrayed himself in his royal robes, took his seat upon [his] throne, and addressed an*

oration to them. And the assembled people shouted, it is the voice of a god, and not of a man! And at once an angel of the Lord smote him and cut him down, because he did not give God the glory (the preeminence and kingly majesty that belong to Him as the supreme ruler); and he was eaten by worms and died.

–Acts 12:21-23, AMP

The passage of Scripture above is definitely another example of an earthly king undermining the authority of the heavenly king. Now, we must understand God's authority is the adhesive that holds the whole of creation together. It is what supports the balance, order and harmony in creation.

Without authority there would be nothing but chaos of eternal proportions. Order is an intricate character of God. Wherever God is there is order. This is why one of the ways to know if God is in charge is to check whether or not there is divine order. So anything that tries to put a dent on God's authority is tampering with the very balance, order and harmony of creation in heaven and earth. The one always responsible for contemptuously testing God's authority is the devil himself. This is why undermining authority under any circumstance is a devilish undertaking.

God's throne is established on eternal authority. Challenging God's authority is somewhat of an existential threat. That is why God brutally deals with any action that is borne out of contempt for His authority. Again, I say, in matters of authority, there are no lines that cannot be crossed and no walls that cannot be breached.

Another example I would like us to consider seriously is the little drama that transpired between pharaoh and God - with Moses and the people of Israel in between.

CHOICE

The Bible says,

'But the Lord hardened Pharaoh's heart, and he would not let them go'

—Exodus 10:27

The first question one might ask after reading the verse of Scripture above is: is God such a *sadistic manipulator?* The answer upfront even as we consider why, is, no!

Why would God harden Pharaoh's heart? Was it so that Pharaoh would not let His people go? Well, let's consider the reason together:

The word *'hardened'* in the Hebrew is *chazaq* (pronounced Khazakh) and it means to causatively strengthen, to fasten upon etc. It basically connotes reinforcing that which already exists. We must therefore not erroneously assume that it was God who initiated the hardening of Pharaoh's heart because this would essentially violate the nature and integrity of His divine justice – there would be no justice in God hardening Pharaoh's heart and afflicting the whole of Egypt on account of Pharaoh's obstinacy.

The hardening of Pharaoh's heart was initiated by Pharaoh and consolidated by God. By an act of God's sovereignty, Pharaoh's resolve not to let the people of Israel go was strengthened. By so doing God removed from Pharaoh's heart the restraint that makes kings tamper justice with mercy – effectively unleashing Pharaoh to explore the depths and heights of wickedness – to his undoing! Pharaoh was repeatedly prevailed upon (Exodus chapters 7–9) to let the people of Israel go but his obstinacy was brazen. So God sovereignly fastened upon the resolve in Pharaoh's heart to make it 'harder'. It was on the basis of this that God could punish Pharaoh and the whole of Egypt.

God could harden Pharaoh's heart because it was in His hand.

He could interfere with Pharaoh's decisions and choices as long as they touched on His authority. He did not influence Pharaoh's personal choices like choosing to worship Him as his God for instance, that was something completely left for Pharaoh to decide. God strictly steered clear Pharaoh's personal matters but kept a keen eye on his kingdom matters.

God's influence stops outside the shores of our personal choices. The King of kings does not meddle with our personal issues. The best He does is to guide us, if we let Him. He gives us enough latitude to decide to either acknowledge His kingship personally or not. Now our choosing to submit to Him does not improve Him in any way for He is all perfect and complete, all by Himself. It does not boost His Godhood.

That a blind man cannot see sunlight does not mean that the sun does not exist. The sun does not exist only in His visual world. That's how any man whose life is not in alignment with God's authority is: God does not exist only in His subjective universe. It does not in the slightest way possible change the higher reality of God's existence in the entire universe.

Having established from God's word the reason why the king's heart is in God's hand (for the sake of authority), it is still in the king's power to choose whether to worship God or not. So it is with every living soul on earth. The king's heart might be in God's hand, yet it is left for the king to choose whether or not to give God his heart. This still boils down to the most important power on earth – the power of choice.

I have had to touch on this aspect to clear every form of ambiguity around this vital truth: that nothing happens in the course of a person's life by accident. Every aspect of the outcome of a person's life is driven by the momentum of choice. Life is God's greatest gift to man but choice is the most important power

God has given to man. So that He Himself stands on queue waiting for how we decide to use it. This proves the simple fact that God is not an insecure despot who gets edgy any time He is not in charge. No, He lets us enjoy the absolute prerogative that the power of choice makes available. Again, forcing us to His will would be tantamount to tyranny. Tyranny is an advanced form of witchcraft. Our God is too eternally holy and secure to condescend to witchcraft.

What then is the best way to deal with earthly authority that is flagrantly evil and causes you so much pain, like the case of Pharaoh who unleashed untold torment on the people of Israel in Egypt? The answer is not to rise in arms but to rise in prayer to Heaven's Great Monarch who dispenses justice to the kings and rulers of the earth! It might take a while, but God always comes through.

CHAPTER FOUR

JESUS CHOSE

Let this same attitude and purpose and [humble] mind be in you which was in Christ Jesus: [Let Him be your example in humility:] Who, although being essentially one with God and in the form of God [possessing the fullness of the attributes which make God God], did not think this equality with God was a thing to be eagerly grasped or retained, But stripped Himself [of all privileges and rightful dignity], so as to assume the guise of a servant (slave), in that He became like men and was born a human being. And after He had appeared in human form, He abased and humbled Himself [still further] and carried His obedience to the extreme of death, even the death of the cross!

—Philippians 2:5-8, AMP

The story of God's redemption of man continues in the New Testament with the Immaculate Conception and birth of Jesus Christ who, though, was born as flesh and blood did not partake in the fall that came as a result of the choice Adam made in the beginning in the Garden of Eden. His flesh was fabricated in the womb of the Virgin Mary, but His life was not powered by the seed of man. He was hewn from a different source. He would be the first and last man to be born naturally but conceived supernaturally. He was supernaturally conceived by the Holy Spirit and was left to undergo all the processes of development until He had fully acquired flesh and blood to be born like every other man. At His birth, He became God's template and prototype for the new creation.

The portion of Scripture quoted above captures at a glance all the choices Jesus made and the things He had to give up and suffer as a result of the choices He made. He was hundred percent God and a hundred percent man. Being hundred percent human, He partook in the full range of the human experience, without sinning. He could get hungry like every man, get tempted by the devil like every man, could feel pain like every man and could be at only one place at a time. He abandoned, so to speak His exalted throne in heaven to take on the overwhelming frailties of the human nature. He lived each day of His life yielding to God so He would fulfill the task He came to earth for. His humility is a feat unbeatable in heaven and on earth.

Being fully God and fully man placed Jesus between two contrary natures. Every day to Him was a battle of choice between His human and divine sides. God put all His hopes for man's redemption on Jesus – just like He placed His faith in Adam in the Garden of Eden. The success or failure of the birth of the new creation depended on Him. Yes, the destiny of the whole human race hung on the balance of His choice. Through Him, God planned on achieving a total reset of the human race – to give every man and woman, boy and girl the opportunity to lay hold of the eternal life Adam and Eve gambled away in the Garden of Eden. This means undoing the mistakes of Adam in the Garden depended on Him. The expiry date to Adam's choices were largely going to be determined by His choices to make the records straight once and for all. To undo the disobedience of Adam, He had to choose to be obedient to God to the death. Oh, yes, it was not going to be a half-hearted undertaking. The right choice for

Jesus was going to involve the spilling of His own blood - sacrificing His own life!

Jesus was God in the flesh with the singular task of rewriting the history of mankind by succeeding in every aspect that Adam failed. To do this, He had to conquer by absolute obedience to God and complete alignment to and execution of His will. That's why He had to live each day on His toes, learning obedience by the things He suffered. Obedience was not preprogrammed into His system simply because He was the God-man. He had to go through life's school of unpleasantness, and had to take it one lesso at a time (Hebrews 5:8).

He was not like *Don Quixote* who was an unpragmatic revolutionary championing hopeless causes. He did not have illusions of grandeur and His reality was not grounded in phantasmal exospheres. He was simply the real deal, every inch God and every width man. He was so ordinary in His conduct that those around Him could easily mistake Him for a mere mortal but had a depth of essence and character substructure that defied the best of human genius and the worst of human problems. His reality was grounded in the Highest (God Almighty) but He could come as low as identifying with and consorting with His own creation; deliberately giving up His super dimensional glory and excellency to imbibe the drabness of the human experience. His secret was simple: though cloaked by the full weight of the human condition and its attendant limitations, His operations were completely powered by the extraterrestrial, superhuman life that He bore within Himself - the same life by which He was conceived without the mortal agency of a man's seed. This phenomenon was what made Him the prototype species and template of the new creation.

To save the human race, He had to deign Himself. He could

not have satisfactorily championed God's cause of the total redemption of mankind without being one hundred percent human. In other words, He had to lead by example. Otherwise, His redemption plan would be of no consequence to the human race.

From the day Jesus gained consciousness of Himself as a human being He began to deliberately choose to obey God. The task before Him was grand and needed practical obedience to God one day at a time to fulfill it. Born into a family that subsisted somewhere at the bottom of society, He grew up learning the trade of His foster father Joseph and became a carpenter, learned Jewish law thoroughly and remained subjected to the authority of His eartly parents until the time of His launch into public ministry.

The Bible records that Jesus grew in wisdom and stature and in favour with God and man (Luke 2: 52). For the first thirty years of His life, He was completely anonymous and practically invisible, gaining ground in the spirit by leading a quiet peasant life. Nothing spectacular was recorded of Him in Scripture in the space of those years, apart from a little encounter He had with the doctors of the law in the temple at the age of twelve in which He silenced them with the high voltage of wisdom that came from His twelve-year-old lips.

Those thirty years were years of spiritual investment, building capacity for an assignment with global and eternal consequence. He was the main theme of all the prophecies that the men of old declared. He was the very peak of what began with Abraham and He polarized history into events that happened before His birth and after His death. Volumes of the books that captured the sacred speakings of God through the ages testified about His greatness. His mortal frame so concealed His divinity that He did not gain any celebrity recognition from Nazareth. He was gold covered in hay – Lord of all clad in the banality of human flesh.

Jesus was tempted at all points like every other man. He had many opportunities to cut corners and run away from troubles: He was tempted to lie, cheat, fornicate, nurse bitterness against cruel folks and all much more of that sort of stuff but chose to yield to the working of the God in Him to remain the unblemished Lamb of God that would take away the sins of the world.

Satan didn't make it any easier as he started attacking from the very day Jesus opened his eyes in the manger. Satan hurled his choicest arsenal at Him. He tampered with the elements, stirred the hearts of the Pharisees against Him, goaded every one close enough to hurt Him, but Jesus remained unshaken and undefeated.

Shortly before He began His public ministry, Jesus was led by the Holy Spirit into the wilderness where the devil presented many choices to Him against God. When Jesus began His public ministry He selected twelve disciples to work with Him. Satan possessed the heart of Judas and made it poised for betrayal against Jesus. Shortly before He went to the cross, Satan possessed Peter's vocal cord to once again present Jesus with the alternative of boycotting the cross. Even while on the cross Satan possessed the onlookers and one of the criminals serving the death sentence with him to taunt Him and, through it all, Jesus remained faithful to the choice He had made to right all the wrongs of Adam and start a new race

Jesus spent His thirty-three and a half years on earth making choices. If it was not choosing to point people to God after performing every miracle instead of taking all the glory, it was choosing to forgive all those that hurt Him. In fact there was not a thing He did without receiving an express okay from God. He declared without shame that everything He did was inspired by God's endless and matchless wisdom and reinforced by God's power.

Though He was equal with God, He did not consider His equality with God as a right that needed to be grasped. He chose to make Himself of no reputation to the point of dying an ignoble death on the cross. His coming to earth was a choice. He had the opportunity to renege on His commitment to redeem mankind and pivot many times but He chose to stick to it at great personal peril. The life and times of Jesus on earth were a lyric of choices.

I personally believe that the most critical time in the life of Jesus was not when He was gasping for life on the cross but when He chose to submit Himself at Gethsemane to the inglorious process that would secure the redemption of mankind. Gethsemane means oil press - it was a place where the labour pains for the new creation began - a metaphorical representation of the process Jesus was to go through for the birth of the new creation. In a typical oil press, an olive oil press for instance, tender and beautiful raw olive fruits are crushed mercilessly, squeezed brutally and pressed offhandedly so that their contents (olive oil) can be extracted to create a product that can both delight the palate and deliver ecstasy to the nostrils. The process of crushing oil condiments in order to process them to oil is usually ruthless and gory but the end result is usually picturesque.

Jesus' soul underwent tough squeezing by the crushing weight of the sins of mankind, past, present and future so that the 'oil' required for the birthing of the new creation could be extracted. In Bible symbolism, oil represents the Spirit. Prior to the death of Jesus, the Holy Spirit was not readily available and accessible to all flesh. After the death of Jesus Christ, His Spirit - the Holy Spiritbecame accessible to all who believe, like a free to air TV channel. In the Godhead, the Holy Spirit is the custodian and dispenser of the divine life of God, available to all who believe and fully paid for by the tough choice Jesus made at Gethsemane. In a sense, the Holy Spirit was poured forth and made available to all who believe on account of the pressing, squeezing and crushing of Jesus Christ on the cross!

Jesus gave up His precious life as a seed so that the new creation could sprout from the same. Thus, ending millennia of death, darkness, degeneration and malignant hopelessness and helplessness that plagued the human race. The chokehold of the devil was broken when Jesus died the vicarious death for mankind.

Gethsemane was where Jesus made the greatest choice in His life on earth. The whole of creation pulsated with anxiety as Jesus knelt to pray. The sweltering tension that built-up in His soul made His sweat as thick as blood. Before Him were two choices:

1. Refuse to go through with the task of saving mankind.
2. Submit to God's will (and die) and go through an inglorious process that would culminate in death on the cross.

The former choice was the easier way out, but He knew better. The Bible says;

> *'And He was withdrawn from them about a stone's throw, and He knelt down and prayed saying; "Father, if it is your will, take this cup away from me; nevertheless not my will but yours, be done"'.*
>
> **—Luke 22:41-42**

I believe this was the toughest choice Jesus ever made while on earth. It was painful in the short run but eternally profitable in the long run. Jesus kept choosing to do God's will until He drew His last breath on the cross. But by the tough choice He made, God's redemption plan would suffer no loss.

With all that Jesus went through, He became qualified to

become God's first born Son in the new creation - a sort of template and standard for anyone who chooses to become a part of the new creation. Jesus was given a name higher than every name mentioned in heaven and earth. He came, He saw, He conquered, and that's why the Bible says,

> *'Looking away (from all that will distract) to Jesus, who is the leader and the source of our faith (giving the first incentive for our belief) and is also its finisher (bringing it to maturity and perfection). He, for the joy (of obtaining the prize) that was set before Him, endured the cross, despising and ignoring the shame and is now seated at the right hand of the throne of God.'*
>
> **–Hebrews 12:2, AMP**

If you read the accounts of Matthew (26:26), Luke (22:41) and Mark (14:32) on the travail of Jesus in Gethsemane, they only mention Gethsemane as a place. In John's account however in John 18:1, the Bible specifically mentions that Gethsemane is actually a garden. So, this is why it is popularly referred to as the Garden of Gethsemane. This is interesting because the first man, Adam, made a choice that sentenced humankind to the gallows in the Garden of Eden. While the second man, Jesus, made a choice that overturned the death sentence hanging on the human race in the Garden of Gethsemane. They both made destinyshaping choices in gardens. The story of redemption therefore stretches from the Garden of Eden to the Garden of Gethsemane!

Jesus did not only heal the sick, cleanse the lepers, raise the dead and free all those who were oppressed of the devil, He chose!Though He was God manifested in the flesh, He engaged the power of choice embedded in His humanity to do the will of God to the death. He happens to be our perfect example - the author and finisher of our faith.

Chapter Five

LAMP AND LIGHT: THE CURE FOR INDECISION

'Your word is a lamp to my feet and a light to my path'

—Psalms 119:105, AMP

Life is a journey whose end is hinged on the choices made. Every human being on earth is a traveller. How we choose to make our journey in time determines our destination in eternity. Only stillborns and babies who die prematurely before the age of accountability are excused from making choices because they leave the earth too soon to have the chance to exercise their will in a destiny-shaping way.

Every traveller needs victuals and a definite destination in mind. In life, all the bus stops, vehicles in which we travel, the people we travel with and all the modalities required to make our journey a complete experience are determined by the choices we make. See, the great script called destiny that God Himself wrote to be uniquely fulfilled by every soul on earth requires the deliberate exercise of the will through making choices to become a reality. We don't get to choose our beginning - who our parents and siblings are, the communities we are born into and where we spend our formative years but we get to choose our ending - the friends we make, the careers we choose and the spouse we marry, the places we live, the number of children we raise etc. Therefore the formative years of our lives when we are at the mercy of the choices of our parents and caregivers as the case may be, are sharply balanced out with the longer years we spend making our own choices.

I must reiterate that God has not destined anyone on earth for destruction. As a matter of truth He has abundantly made it clear that,

> *'for I know the thoughts and plans that I have for you, says the Lord, thoughts and plans for welfare and peace and not for evil, to give you hope in your final outcome.'*
>
> **—Jeremiah 29:11, AMP**

True as this might be, God does not force anyone's hand to fulfill the good and wonderful plans He has for them. And just as He has good plans, so does the devil have evils plans - and also, fulfilling God's good plans or the devil's evil plans solely depends on the determinant choices we make.

God, for instance, did not create Judas Iscariot to be Jesus' betrayer and end up committing suicide by hanging himself. I make bold to say that Judas chose to cooperate with the devil to make a mess of his life and make him epitomise treachery, greed and apostasy. The following few verses convince me so:

> *Then one of the Twelve [apostles], who was called Judas Iscariot, went to the chief priests and said, What are you willing to give me if I hand Him over to you? And they weighed out for and paid to him thirty pieces of silver [about twenty-one dollars and sixty cents]. AND FROM THAT MOMENT HE SOUGHT A FITTING OPPORTUNITY TO BETRAY HIM.* **(emphasis added)**
>
> **—Matthew 26:14-15, AMP**

CHOICE

The betrayal of Jesus was a prophecy as sure as His birth but its fulfilment was entirely dependent on anyone who made the choice to so do. In other words, fulfilling evil and good prophecies don't just happen by fluke, they happen by deliberate choosing. For Judas, it took cold, tactical, calculated and deliberate strategizing and double-checking of stratagems to betray Jesus. He, like the remaining eleven disciples had the chance to bounce the devil off him by saying a choice NO! But he didn't. He opened the door of his heart to cheap greed and costly treachery which earned him doom and one of the aliases of the antichrist: the son of perdition (John 17:12). Can you imagine someone who was as close to Jesus to be called His disciple ending up as the son of perdition? All because he chose an undertaking that would cost him His very soul!

Now it is imperative for me to stress that making choices most times doesn't come easy, especially when it touches on very critical and highly crucial issues. I am talking about when the alternatives on ground are not just dual but multiple and are of seemingly equal heft and importance as the right choice. One is thrown under severe pressure and struggles to withstand the crushing weight of uncertainty when they are to choose from several options.

To iron this out, we must first understand what a 'right choice is'. A right choice is a choice that when made draws a person closer to God and makes them fulfill His will for their life. A right choice therefore is beyond human perspective and judgment, both of which are limited. It is something that should synchronize with God's judgment and perspective. For what is right in the sight of man might be dead wrong in the sight of God. That's why Scripture establishes that the way that seems right to a man will lead him to destruction. Fleeing from obeying God's command to go preach in Nineveh and heading to Tarshish seemed right in Jonah's eyes but it landed him in a three-day sepulchral hibernation in the belly of a fish. In the light of being in Christ, making a choice is not enough, making the right choice is what counts.

Many people today complain of not knowing what to do and not even knowing which way to go. I know I speak of a large chunk of the society. It's okay to be confused once in a while but it's not okay to walk with God and still grope in darkness and confusion. For the Bible says,

> *'God is light, and there is no darkness in Him at all (no, not in any way).'*
>
> **–1 John 1:56, AMP**

Darkness is a result of the absence or insufficiency of light. Confusion in life comes as a result of not allowing His light permeate our will. Only a will illumined by God can make the right choices. A proof of growth in our relationship with God is that we easily discern and set out to execute His will. The Bible speaks distinctively of God thus,

> *'Every good gift and every perfect (free, large, full) gift is from above; it comes down from the father of all (that gives) light, in (the shining of) whom there can be no variation (rising or setting) or shadow cast by His turning (as an eclipse)'*
>
> **–James 1:17, AMP**

This simply means that God is not only eternal but eternally stable. There no ups and downs, highs and lows with Him; there is only stability and unquenching brightness. Every life that is truly in His care should reflect those.

Many people waste precious time and opportunities not

because they don't want to be poised for prompt making of right choices but because there is an iron clad disease that chips away at their will slowly and steadily like a fire fanned by little or no breeze. This malaise is called indecision, and it arises from a chronic case of not knowing what choices to make per time to propel one farther in the direction of God's will for their life. This further leads to double mindedness. And on this the Bible declares,

> *'God is light, and there is no darkness in Him at all (no, not in any way).'*

> **–James 1:8, AMP**

Such a person is like a shooting star, unsuitable to sustain and reflect God's glorious light to the darkened world. I call such a person a flash in the pan of history, so swift yet unfit. God does not handover sensitive issues to unstable people for they will throw them to the gutter at the slightest stir of a whim. Impulsiveness is evidence enough that a person is still immature.

One does not necessarily always need the guidance of God to make a choice that would earn them some profit in this life. But to make a choice that will strike a chord in eternity, a person must need God more than they need oxygen. The world is full of darkness. Only God has the true light that can light every man. We as God's people have a great a privilege given to us by Him to navigate the labyrinths of life's course and emerge victorious in the afterlife. Making us both relevant on earth and in heaven. This privilege is nothing but God's word. God's word happens to be put together for us today as the Bible to aid us in our journey through life on earth.

The psalmist says God's word is a lamp to his feet and a light to his path. That means God's word guides his feet in taking the right steps and illuminates his path so that he can know which way to go. No one dares travel without light; anybody who tries it probably is disaster-hungry. No! Not on land or by sea. This is because light aids vision, vision means visibility, without which is gross darkness. All the wonderful colours and scenic sights of nature become useless in the dark. There is no poetry in the dark, only dolorous chimes and moments. God's word is loaded with God's thoughts. God's word is God Himself.

> *Jesus said, "Man shall not live and be upheld and sustained by bread alone, but by every word that comes forth from the mouth of God",*
>
> **–Matthew 4:4, AMP**

That means God's word is food for the soul. Now the little problem that exists in eating God's word is that one must be ready to go beyond the surface of words printed in ink on pages of paper to touch the pulse of inspiration which makes the Bible the only valid container of God's spoken word and all time best seller on earth, or be left with nothing but novel words and ideas replete with the inability to transform, impart life and inspire.

That's why a professor or scholastic genius can do a classic masterpiece exegesis on the Bible without touching the author of the Bible – the Holy Spirit. To eat God's word, the printed words must usher the reader to the powerful unprinted words which come out directly from the mouth of God to the heart of the reader or listener.

The Bible is the compendium of God's will and counsel in a general sense. To get His mouth-to-mouth word to us, we must have a functional relationship with the Holy Spirit. A healthy relationship with the Holy Spirit reflects on how much light and practical nourishment one gets from the written word. God's speakings through the ages have been consistent, He spoke volumes and still speaks volumes today. He spoke to the saints of old, directing them on what to do, He still speaks today and can still speak today to you and me to both light up our feet and paths. God's word is potent and powerful and pierces through the darkness like a burning shaft. The first thing God's word does when we open our hearts to Him is to put an end to the internal darkness by renewing and transforming a person from within – putting a halt to all forms of ambiguity and making God's will crystal clear.

The entrance of God's word into the heart of a seeker of truth either by study or instruction administers light and understanding (Psalm 119:130). God is light (1 John 1:5). This means light is an integral part of His material essence; a motif of His frame. God is not like light. He is light! God's word is God (John 1:1). It is for this reason God's word releases light anywhere it makes an entry by the mighty working and power of the Holy Spirit. Again, the one who ensures this happens is the Holy Spirit.

Now, whether by personal study or by listening to the teaching and preaching of God's word, light only comes when God's word enters a person's heart. A proof that God's light is present is that understanding is furnished. This is beyond printed letters and spoken words – it is a direct transmission of the essential substance of God to man by the Holy Spirit. This is why I would like to reiterate reading the Bible or listening to a preacher does not necessarily lead to the receipt of light and understanding. God's word is not a dark code that should be deciphered. It is spirit matter that must be revealed by the Holy Spirit.

The Bible says,

> *"Every Scripture is God-breathed (given by His inspiration) and profitable for instruction, for reproof and conviction of sin, for correction of error and discipline in obedience, [and] for training in righteousness (in holy living, in conformity to God's will in thought, purpose, and action), so that the man of God may be complete and proficient, well fitted and thoroughly equipped for every good work."*
>
> **—2 Timothy 3:16-17, AMP**

The word Scripture in the Greek is graphe (prounced grafay) and it means a written document, a Holy Writ (writings and sayings of an authority [God is the highest authority –Luke 1:35; Ephesians 4:6] that cannot be challenged) and this is basically an immutable document that must be diligently consulted to guide the believer's journey of faith.

From the passage above, it is clear that Scripture is the centre of God's dealings with the believer. This is like the constitutions of nations today by which governments and political entities are administered. For instance, the constitution of the Federal Republic of Nigeria is the document that guides all operations within the political entity called Nigeria. The government, governance and citizens of Nigeria are all guided by the constitution. Anything done outside the provisions of the constitution is termed unconstitutional! It is the constitutions of nations today that make them different from the barbarian cities of centuries past.

The difference between Scripture and the constitutions of nations is that Scripture is God-breathed (given by His inspiration) while nations' constitutions are man-formulated. The breath of God is actually the Spirit of God. This means the Holy Spirit is the author of the written word. God is not the author of confusion. If He has authored the Bible He would inspire and empower believers to live by it, not operate beyond it! A significant difference between the Christian faith system and other religions out there is the Christian Scripture! And this is because it is the only book under heaven that testifies of the kingship and lordship of Jesus Christ (John 5: 9).

A lot of people fail to execute God's will because they do not even know it to begin with. So the devil cashes in on their ignorance of God's will to make a mess of their lives. Their choices become a pile of haphazard arrangements without the requisite knowledge of God's word. His will remains a mystery and when His will remains a mystery, a person's life becomes a knotty misery.

A rich, prayerful ingestion and digestion of God's word brings stability to the mind by dealing endless death blows to the virus of indecision until stability and light are restored to a person's mind. Prayer makes the heart ready to receive God's word and cracks the shell of printed letters and spoken words, so the heart can lay hold of the substance of God's word which brings assurance and peace, and decimates uncertainty. When this happens a person begins to acquire God's stability steadily. God's word ceases to become a well-edited printed work or beautifully preached sermon. It becomes something personal that God speaks to a person. It is on this note that a person becomes so skilful with God's word they do not only pray for what they want but what He wants, which leaves most of their life's questions answered.

A person who knows God's will can dare the impossible and still emerge victorious. Daniel and his friends kept defying the laws of Babylon without having a hair on their skin broken because they knew His will concerning matters. May the Lord ignite a wild hunger and passion for His word in your heart today in Jesus name!

Prayer and God's word must go together like wood and fire, like hammer and nail. One without the other leads to incompleteness and deficiency. No one has ever won a race by running on one foot and no one can clap with one hand! Yes, no one can get the best of God's word without prayer and no one can get the best of prayer without God's word!

A prayerfully word-driven Christian life is like a car moving at top speed on a full tank in the right direction. All the details and solutions to life's complexities are wrapped up in God's word. God's word does not only quench the darkness within, it also empowers one to vanquish the surrounding darkness. A prayerfully word-driven life does not know gravity and all its rules. That change you seek begins with saturating your mind with God's word. It might be slow but it is sure. Paul implores thus;

> *"Do not be conformed to this world (this age), (fashioned after and adapted to its external, superficial customs), but be transformed (changed by the (entire), renewal of your mind (by its new ideals and its new altitude) so that you may prove (yourself) what is the good and acceptable and perfect will of God, even the thing which is good and acceptable and perfect (in His sight for you)'.*
>
> **–Romans 12:2, AMP**

When there is a healthy dose of prayer and God's word in a person's life, they have a rich supply of the understanding of God's will for their life, they brook no apathy or indecision, they rise up in obedience to God's command always and execute His will without prevarication!

Speaking of lights, we must understand that there are two types of light under heaven:

1. The true light
2. The counterfeit lights

In the beginning was the Word, and the Word was with God, and the Word was God...In Him was life, and the life was the light of men. And the light shines in the darkness, and the darkness did not comprehend it...That was THE TRUE LIGHT which gives light to every man coming into the world. **(emphasis added)**

–John 1:1, 4-5, 9 NKJV

Lucifer was once the consummate embodiment of celestial refulgence – he was an anointed Cherub, and son of the morning whose frame bore and exuded God's light. After going rogue and getting cast out of heaven, Lucifer became the devil forever losing the capacity to bear God's light. So the best he can do now is masquerade and/or transform himself into an angel of light. The

Bible says,

For Satan himself transforms himself into an angel of light (2 Corinthians 11:14, NKJV)

Since Satan has lost the capacity to bear God's light, which by the way is the true light, he has built and perfected his capacity to present counterfeit and/or false light.

Any light that does not have Jesus Christ (who is the word of God, bearer of God's life and the only true light) as its source is counterfeit and/or false.

There are so many systems out there in the world that seem to shine some kinds of light. They shine lights through humanitarian programmes (like those of the United Nations and several NGOs whose core agenda is to obliterate God from society), beautifully crafted philosophies that espouse dependence on oneself instead of God (as contained in many self help and motivational books today), arts, entertainment and culture etc. All lights shine but not all lights are true. Truth is one: Jesus Christ. Jesus Christ is the only true light that bears the substance of God's reality and life and can dispense the same to whoever believes in Him. Actually any light that does not hail from Jesus Christ will yield nothing but wholesale, full-scale darkness!

Three areas God's light must shine on in the life of a believer daily include:

i. The feet (Psalms 119:105) for direction. You walk in the direction of your feet. In the journey of faith direction is key.

ii. The path (Psalms 119:105) for spiritual progress. The path of spiritual progress continually leads you to places in God.

iii. The heart (2 Corinthians 4:6) for the continual knowledge of the glory of God. The heart must be flooded by God's light in order to be filled with the living, functional knowledge of God that can produce fruits in the believer.

Again, the light of God is always produced when the word of God gains entrance into the depths of man (Psalm 119:130). This can only happen when the believer enlarges their appetite for God's word to consume more and more and more and more and some more, in the place of prayer.

CHAPTER SIX

GOD AND SATAN ARE LIMITED

'And the Lord God commanded the man, saying, you may freely eat of every tree of the garden; but of the tree of the knowledge of good and evil and blessing and calamity you shall not eat, for in the day that you eat of it you shall surely die'.

—Genesis 2:16-17, AMP

'But the serpent said to the woman, you shall not surely die, for God knows that in the day you eat of it your eyes will be opened, and you will be like God, knowing the difference between good and evil and blessing and calamity'

—Genesis 3:4-5, AMP

God said 'No'. Satan said 'Go'. God said, 'Eat and die'. Satan said, 'Eat and fly'. But I humbly submit that neither God nor the devil could determine man's choice. They both laid out an option that had attendant consequences. That was it. Nothing more, nothing less. Neither God nor Satan pushed man's will. Now their methods are very different in that God is righteously direct in His dealings with man while Satan has the virtues of a snake - windy, cold and deceptive. But it is still up to man to choose to yield to God's righteous directness or Satan's wily deception.

Christians often say silly stuff like, 'It's the devil's work, I don't know how it happened, it was the devil that pushed me etc.' This is very mistaken because Christians who pass blames to the devil simply give him the power he does not have, perhaps because they prefer to live in denial and irresponsibility than own up to their mistakes. A person who gets caught red-handed stealing and yells shamelessly, 'It was the devil that pushed me' is simply giving the devil credit for their action. No matter how horrible their situation is, someone has passed through something similar or much worse and still made the right choice. And that is enough to not excuse their action. By the way, actions are products of carefully thought and processed choices. The man who does not steal under harsh financial pressure chooses not to, and the man who resorts to stealing chooses to do so. There is no truth to the statement: 'I have no choice'. I dare say that no challenge in the realm of man today is unprecedented! Someone, somewhere, somehow and at some point in time has experienced it with a testimony of victory – His name is Jesus Christ! There is no temptation that cannot be overcome. This is especially true because our Lord and Master Jesus Christ went through every point of test, trial, tribulation and temptation designed to take advantage of the frailties of the human nature and did not fall one time. He overcame them all. This is why He is the template for our faith (Hebrews 12:2). Jesus was and still is simply impeccable and flawless. The Bible speaks of Him thus:

For we do not have a high priest who is unable to sympathize with our weaknesses, but we have one who has been tempted in every way, just as we are – yet was without sin.

–Hebrews 4:15, NIV

That He did it successfully under the full weight of the limitations of the human condition is proof enough that it can be done. Does this mean that those who falter, fail, break, fold, melt, crater and breakdown under the full weight of the limitations of the human condition have become complete write-offs and failures? The answer is a capital NO! God does not expect machine or algorithmic perfection from the Christian who is on pilgrimage through the world's hostile terrain, heaven-bound. As long as the Christian's eyes are on Jesus, victory is sure. In times of unintentional failings, the Bible clearly admonishes all believers to:

> *...approach the throne of grace with confidence, so that we may receive mercy and find grace to help us in our time of need.*
>
> **—Hebrews 4:16, NIV**

Obedience to God and yielding to the devil's deception are choices. I am not talking about living by the power of the will here. For the Christian life cannot be lived on the strength of the will but by the power of the Holy Spirit at work within a believer. But the power of the Holy Spirit only works in conjunction with choices made. The Holy Spirit does not infringe on a man's power of choice. This is why walking with Him requires choosing to daily obey His command and follow His lead. The Holy Spirit will not force a man to go West if the man has already chosen to go East. Though He won't hesitate to let the man know he is supposed to go West.

We must live each day of our lives understanding and appreciating the fact that God has given us a tremendous power which He expects us to use to positively affect our lives. Also, with great power comes great responsibility - just as He has given us the power, He expects us to learn its use and work in conjunction with His grace to avoid the curses that abound when not used properly.

We must also understand that Satan cannot take what he is not given. Yes, he is a thief who takes more than what he is given but does not take what he is not given either deliberately or carelessly. Given a plot of land, he takes a whole city but given no place at all he remains an incapacitated and emasculated spirit floating in mid-air, a vagabond of sorts without a base to call his own. There is no more space in heaven for Satan and his demon legions as you read this (Revelation 12:8). His memory and DNA have been forever obliterated from heaven. It is therefore impossiblefor Satan to take even a one-trillionth fraction of inch of heaven.

However, if given just a tiny space, he exercises his capacity for thievery and takes up as much as he can without the owner's knowledge. This is proven in his hostile takeover of the whole earth when Adam gave him something as small as a choice. His (Satan's) goal was to besiege the whole earth. He wanted to break the order in creation and subject it to the bondage of corruption but needed the keys to gain legal access to the earth's potentials under the care of Adam. So he came up with a plan and design for the ultimate corruption of man which he packaged as a great suggestion and sold it to man, though not without first deceiving man's companion – the woman. This thus became the genesis of what we now know as the old creation which is completely unacceptable in the sight of God.

The old creation was birthed by choice. The new creation was also birthed by choice. Today every man or woman born into the world is born as an old creature which is bereft of God's life and essentially sinful by default as a result of one choice Adam mode. In other words every man or woman was born a sinner by default.

CHOICE

It takes choice to become a new creature in Christ. This means it is man's power to decide whether or not he wants to continue living by default or by choice.

A lot of people today live by default and expect things to magically change or swing in their favour. They even go as far as trying to blame the heavens for the unfortunate outcome of their lives. Listen friend, it takes choice to live by default just as it takes choice to live by choice.

Once a boy or girl reaches the age accountability, they have reached the fork in the road of their life's journey. And by choices they choose the path to take and make life-defining and lifeshaping decisions. It does not matter where one is at the moment - on the mountain top or in the valley, in the pool of comfort or in the jaws of pain; there is always a choice to make. As long as one draws breath, they can make a choice.

The Almighty God in heaven is all powerful and His might is beyond calculation. He rules over the affairs of men on earth and dictates the interplay among the elements of creation. Satan, who is the cosmic felon awaiting the judgment meted him in heaven to be established on earth is also powerful to some degree; he champions the course of evil and corruption throughout the universe. Both God and Satan seek to interact with the realm of man for different reasons. They put the power in their disposal to great use in order to achieve this. Yet their powers do not prevail in any man's life until he has made a choice to permit them so.

It takes choice to be under the devil's reign by living in sin. It takes choice also to be endued with power from on high to live above sin. However, the powers of God and Satan are limited by the power of choice given by God to man.

The statements, 'I did not have a choice', 'I do not have a choice' are some of the greatest irresponsible lies told on earth today. No matter how fast it is meant to happen, you and I still have a window of a few seconds to make a choice. Actually the option of choosing right is always given to us even if we do not understand it. Cooperating with Satan by choice on the other hand makes us spiritually obtuse and always makes us choose wrong even if we think we understand it.

Those who choose God are jealously guided and guarded by Him. Misfortune does not befall them because their footsteps are always ordered right by Him. They are not caught in the wrong place at the wrong time. They do not just get knocked down by cars on the streets by accident because of how much they matter to His cause. They are not likely to catch stray bullets and die like mere men or beasts do. They are always on point consciously or unconsciously. All things – good or bad, work together for their good.

Meanwhile, those who choose Satan always live as victims of circumstance. Their souls are almost always in stupor with confusion and uncertainties. They struggle very hard to watch their back and so on. In short they experience the inverted consequences that befall those who choose God.

Choosing God is something done deliberately and actively. While choosing the devil is something that can be done actively or passively. Those who actively choose Satan do so by the power of their will in order to enjoy the bounties in his store yard of corruption. People like this are visibly championing the causes of Satan all around the world today across the different fields of human endeavour. Those who passively choose Satan are those who would not pick courage and dare the odds. They would rather take the path of convenience and live by default. The path of convenience always conjoins with the path of connivance with the devil!

CHOICE

This takes us back our initial lesson on the three categories of trees in the Garden of Eden. Actually those three categories of trees produce three categories of people in the world today.

1. **Those that eat every other tree in the Garden alone:** These are everyday people who choose not to exercise their power of choice but rather live by default. They mark time and place themselves at the mercy of fate. They believe in *que sera sera* (what will be, will be). This category of people choose Satan passively.

2. **Those that eat the tree of the knowledge of good and evil:** These are those who deliberately cut covenant with Satan on earth. It's a *quid pro quo* (transactional; something for something) arrangement they have with the devil in order to flagrantly promote his cause on earth. Some of the things they enjoy at his table include power, fame and fortune. They proudly parade themselves as proponents of Satan's cause on earth.

3. **Those that eat the tree of life:** These are people who actively choose to be with God and submit to His will. Consequent upon their choice of God they are slighted and hated for no just cause in the world. They are not ashamed to represent God in word and deed and champion His cause on earth at the peril of their own lives.

The prostitutes who sell their bodies for money have a choice. The magnates who sell their souls for money have a choice. The saints who sell their souls for eternal life have a choice. Everyone has a choice!

CHAPTER SEVEN

THE WILL OF MAN VERSUS THE WILL OF GOD

The great equation of life is thus:

SITUATION		CHOICE			CONSEQUENCE
Circumstances Temptation Pressure Lack Prosperity Crises etc	+	God's word + God's will + Man's free will	Satan's deceit + Satan's will + Man's Will	➡	Good with God Or Evil with Satan

The above equation shows that choice is central to everything that happens to man on earth. And life is simply a consequence of choices made by the exercise of man's free will in line with God's word and will and/or Satan's deceit and will in response to every situation he finds himself. The consequence ultimately transcends the world and follows man right into the afterlife.

The will of God is the sum total of the things He desires to do and get done. The will of God is clearly expressed in His word. The will of man on the other hand is the sum total of his desires, consent and passion as expressed by his capacity to choose.

CHOICE

Whenever a man exercises his will through actions that place a demand on his capacity or ability to choose, he is said to have made a choice.

Man's will is free because it is choice-neutral. That is to say it does not sustain any bias for any particular course of action, good or bad. And it is independent of foreign influences. I dare to say the freest thing on earth is not the bird in the sky but the will of man.

The world is a hub of situations. Every man born into the world is born to handle situations which come in different colours, shapes and sizes. Each of these situations requires him to make a choice by exercising his will. Now each of these situations equally has the will of God and the will of Satan. The will of God is expressed in His word. The will of Satan is wound up in his deceit.

Every exercise of man's will results in expressing the will of God or Satan for a particular situation depending on the choice made. It takes partnership between the will of man and the will of God to birth the kingdom of God on earth. It also takes partnership between the will of man and the will of Satan to birth the kingdom of darkness on earth.

In partnering with God's will, a man's will must be exercised within the ambit of God's word - which is simply a compendium of God's counsel, will and purpose. Now God's word is the skeletal framework upon which His will is established. Man's will must be fluid and malleable enough to take the shape of the mould of God's will. This takes time and patience in practice.

In such a partnership, God's will is the perfect, immutable half. Man's will is the inferior, crude half needing pruning and more pruning. As the man continues in a submissive relationship with God by daily choosing to be under God, his will gains alignment. God's will inches through and permeates man's will, ridding it of human excesses. This is seen in the man's choices being informed by God's will as contained in His word.

Gradually, the man ceases to make hasty, impulsive decisions. He begins to make choices that bear positive decisions. He begins to make choices that bear positive eternal consequences. And ultimately the *versus factor* between the will of God and the will of man disappears completely. What results is the unification of the will of God and the will of man. In other words, the will of God and the will of man become one. For such a life, Satan is deleted and the equation of life is rewritten thus:

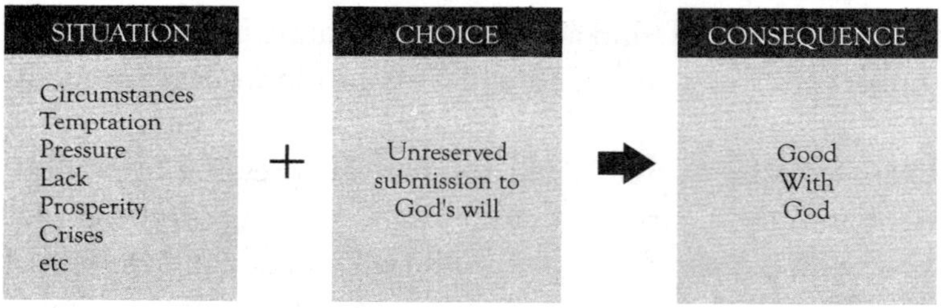

A man whose life is in line with the equation above exercises his free will in line with God's will. The outcome of his entire life is engineered by the will of God. His choices: who he marries, career, business, friends, time management, use of resources, remaining faithful to God in the face of danger and austerity, forgiving hurt, loving in spite of being hated, being truthful even if it means losing favours and so forth, all harp God's will to the world.

May the *versus factor* between our will and will of God give way so that our lives will be the express manifestation of His counsel in Jesus name!

CHAPTER EIGHT

CHOOSE LIFE, DEATH IS NOT WORTH IT

Life and death are on the two extremes of life's balance as always sandwiched by the choices man makes through the exercise of his free will. This can be simply illustrated thus:

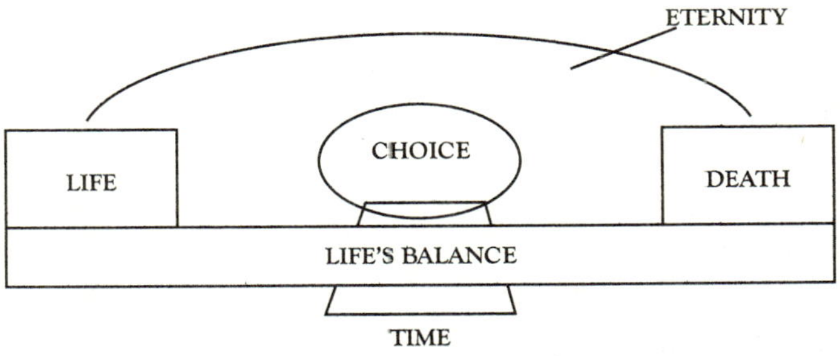

By choosing life or death, we do not mean choosing to live or to die as merely as the words imply. Life and death in context here refer to something much bigger than drawing breath or giving up the ghost. In the New Testament, the sum total of life is God and the sum total of death is the absence of Him. To gain life means to ultimately gain God and to gain death is to lose Him ultimately.

Every human being on earth today is born in time to make their journey to the two extremes of eternity. This journey is powered by the choices one makes. This means the moment a man or woman, boy or girl reaches the age of accountability, the journey begins. This reality cuts across racial barriers, geographical and political disparities, religious beliefs and social orientation. The almost eight billion people populating the planet today are not exempted from this journey. It is an order God Himself has set on earth to which every nation, tribe, tongue and people are subject whether actively or passively, the journey must be made.

I understand there are several religions blasting hard in the world's spiritual stratosphere today with diverse beliefs and philosophies about the afterlife and the way to get there. Now considering these religions and their various belief systems is beyond the scope of our discourse but one thing remains sure, almost every one of these religions has a vague idea about a world apart from the one we live in, a life apart from the one that is lived here and now. Arguments could go on nonstop about the way to the afterlife but arguments themselves do not shape reality.

If anything, arguments blur reality most times and prevent people from reading the truth. The truth is and shall always remain that Jesus is the only way to God and the access route to life eternal because He Himself is the way, truth and life, and this is regardless of what ancient metaphysical scrolls say. I do not even pay mind to whatever any one dead or alive has to say about an alternative route to God apart from Jesus Christ. Truth remains that all routes apart from Jesus Christ lead to eternal death. The choice is there for everyone to make concerning where they would end up eventually in the life after now.

Needful to say, there is a constant principle that underscores the operations of God and the devil. This is what I call the *God-*

one-devil-many principle which basically postulates that, God's option to life is one while the devil's options to death are many. This is both objectively and subjectively so true because God's word concerning every situation we find ourselves is one. He does not say 'yes' in the morning, 'may be' in the afternoon and 'No' in the evening. His word is His bond. The heavens and earth could tremble and fold up but not a word that has proceeded from His mouth can fall to the ground unfulfilled. It is just impossible for God to renege on His word and/or edit it after He has already declared it! What you see and hear is what you get with God.

Meanwhile, the devil is a master of the doublespeak, speaking with many tongues from both sides of his mouth, fraudulently cryptic. He, through subterfuge, makes death-worthy options available to all those who seek them. This goes to mean that the will of Satan is convoluted, windy, complicatedly intertwined and endlessly sinuous. What you see and hear are not what you get with the devil – there is always a hidden clause, undeclared consequence, concealed side effect, etc., with him!

Between the time a person is born and the time before they reach the age of accountability, the road of life's journey is one lane. After which the road diverges at the exact moment they reach the age of accountability. A soul that makes it to this point becomes a matter of special interest to the heavens and a fresh target for the kingdom of darkness. The architecture of the realm of the spirit is such that every male and female in the land of the living is known not just by head count but by the quality of the choices they make. So people are rated not by the number of breaths they take but by the quality of choices they make.

The great general Joshua, Moses' successor came to a critical point in his leadership in which he had to make his followers exercise their free will as touching worship. The sky over Israel was stormy and there was a lot of chaos. Polytheism spread through the land like the Bubonic plague. People were divided in regard to which way to go in terms of worship. Joshua knew he had to use his leadership privilege to make his people responsible for the path they would choose. He did not force his personal choices and preferences down their throat. He simply said,

> *"...And if it seems evil to you to serve the Lord, choose for yourselves this day whom you will serve, whether the gods which your fathers served that were on the other side of the River, or the gods of the Amorites, in whose land you dwell. But as for me and my house, we will serve the Lord."*
>
> **–Joshua 24:15, NKJV**

Note this careful choice of words. When it got to addressing the options before them, he was keen to spell them out as follows:

1. The 'gods' which their fathers served were many
2. The LORD whom himself and family had chosen to serve was one.

Now, notice that this again buttresses the God-one-devil-many principle we have just considered. My dear friend, serving God is a choice and serving the devil is equally a choice. Something worthy of note here is that the power of choice is bestowed upon man by God Himself. Is it not amazing? That the Almighty can choose to be limited by man by empowering Him so? More still, by placing Himself in such a position where He, so to speak, is at the mercy of man's exercise of this same power He has freely given him.

With solemn concentration, let us consider the following portion of scripture together. For emphasis' sake, I would like to quote it in upper case. They are the very words of God Himself concerning this matter:

> *"SEE, I HAVE SET BEFORE YOU TODAY LIFE AND GOOD, DEATH AND EVIL, IN THAT I COMMAND YOU TODAY TO LOVE THE LORD YOUR GOD, TO WALK IN HIS WAYS, AND TO KEEP HIS COMMANDMENTS, HIS STATUTES, AND HIS JUDGMENTS, THAT YOU MAY LIVE AND MULTIPLY; AND THE LORD YOUR GOD WILL BLESS YOU IN THE LAND WHICH YOU GO TO POSSESS. BUT IF YOUR HEART TURNS AWAY SO THAT YOU DO NOT HEAR, AND ARE DRAWN AWAY, AND WORSHIP OTHER GODS AND SERVE THEM, I ANNOUNCE TO YOU TODAY THAT YOU SHALL SURELY PERISH; YOU SHALL NOT PROLONG YOUR DAYS IN THE LAND WHICH YOU CROSS OVER THE JORDAN TO GO IN AND POSSESS."*
>
> **—Deuteronomy 30:15-18, NKJV**

This is a universal call to mankind. It is God's command for all peoples to choose life and good. Choosing life and good means choosing to keep His commandments, statues and judgments. All this is possible only in Christ. It is impossible to choose life and good without first choosing Christ as Lord and personal saviour. It is only in Christ that man can be empowered to please God. No other human formula or arrangement will do

In time we have enough elbow room to make as many choices as possible. But in Christ we know that we have to make choices that have a bearing on eternal life - the choices that truly reflect the content of God's character - the choices that would still hold water in the hereafter. This is because in the final analysis, when all is said and done, we are going to be weighed by the quality of choices we have made in time. That then would determine if we are life-worthy or death worthy.

The devil will stop at nothing to blot out the consciousness of the consequences of our choices in the afterlife. He would try his best to make hearts cold with the gains and pleasures of this life. It is a pity that even believers fall for his deceit. A lot of Christians today are more concerned about their gains and comfort in this life. The afterlife becomes a farfetched dream; an afterthought contemplated upon very once in a while.

Choosing death of course offers quick and instant gratification. It is a quick pain reliever that does not cure the underlying malady. It is almost a magical panacea of sorts: bigger houses, bigger cars, bigger planes, bigger bank accounts, bigger clout, more power, and more things that are designed to satiate the five senses. But the true cry from the implant of eternity in the heart is left unanswered and grotesquely suppressed. Do not get me wrong, wealth and riches are God's will for His people. But God's goal for his people is not things but Him. This is because everything under heaven has a lifespan and is corruptible. So if we spend time investing in things under heaven and give no time to investing in the things which are in heaven, what we are sure to end up with is regret and tears.

'Had I known' is a fool's cry. Wise people trust in God with all their hearts and lean not on their understanding. Their choices are not informed by the seen only. Their choices have a bearing on life. They measure whatever they do by eternity. So that instead of gaining the world they gain their souls and instead of gaining death and evil they gain life and good. Instead of taking the many short cuts to death eternal, they embrace the one and only way to life eternal, Jesus Christ the Lord!

Heed God's command today and choose life every day of your life. For again He has said,

CHOICE

I call heaven and earth to witness this day against you that I have set before you life and death, the blessings and the curses; therefore choose life, that you and your descendants may live.

–Deuteronomy 30:19, AMP

The consequences of our choices affect not only us but our descendants as well. Our descendants here go beyond the fruits of our loins. It means the total number of people whose lives are tied to ours and whose destinies are intertwined with ours. What we do directly or consequently affects them. Their 'living' or 'dying', 'failing' or 'succeeding' depends on the choices we make.

Do you realize how much power God committed to man at all? One Adam and Eve rendered the whole of the human race dead because of one choice they made. Think of how many people would have been lost if the likes of Charles Spurgeon, Martin Luther, Benson Idahosa, Reinhard Bonnke had not chosen to answer God's call. Think of how many people are blessed just because people like Enoch Adeboye rose up. Think of how many people are cursed today because people like Anton Scandon Lavey (founder of the church of Satan, USA) rose up. Think of how many millions of lives are lost today because of the Satanic legacies of Alice Bailey and Margaret Sanger. Then think of how many thousands and millions of lives would be blessed and live if you choose right today. Choose life my friend because in the long run, death is not worth it!

CHAPTER NINE

GOD IS THE GOD OF THE LIVING, NOT THE DEAD

Jesus answered and said to them... "God is not the God of the dead, but of the living,"

—Matt. 22:29, 32, NKJV

Where death ends, life begins. Life does not really begin until a person chooses to accept the divinity and Lordship of Christ. No matter how vivacious and outgoing a person is, and no matter how electrified their environment is, if they are without Christ they are dead. Being born into the land of the living does not mean a person is alive.

It takes more than oxygen to live! It is possible to take lungfuls of air daily and still be dead. Oxygen only powers the body. The spirit of man can only be powered by the Spirit of God who happens to be the very breath of God. A man who lives on oxygen alone is not any different from beasts that roam the earth and insects that flutter and zither in midair. How do you breathe? Do you just breathe? Do you live by the air in the world alone or do you lock lips with your maker and have Him pump life into your inner man?

The greatest paradox on earth today is a *dead life*. It is a life that is characterized by bubbling exterior and cold, lifeless interior.

See, so many people today vibrate with the force of mad-rushing waves but when the dust of activity settles, a gaping emptiness hunts them inside. They are frozen on the inside even though the world around them thaws under the heat of civilization. The spirit of man by design can only receive ventilation from the Spirit of the Most High God. Any other attempt to gain soulish breath would end up a fiasco.

Our days on earth are an infinitesimal part of time and time itself happens to be a speck of floating dust in the light of eternity. If history is anything to go by, mortality is never the answer. This is because the loftiest achievement attained by a mortal would eventually become a memory blown into the gust of oblivion. Time itself has an expiry date in God's grand calendar. Once we exit the earth and emerge on the other side, will we be free to meet the Lord? Or shall we be forever severed from Him consequent upon the choices we made on earth?

Kings have lived and passed on, monuments have been built and have crumbled to dust, human genius has never really provided answers for all of life's questions. The past is inked on pages and we are inspired to leave a mark on earth as we read. No one truly has an answer to the future except the great creator Himself who shall judge all flesh as everything on earth gets cremated in the fullness of time. We are taught by philosophers and poets to etch our indelible mark on the rock plains of time. Little is said about striving to make choices that shall make indelible marks on eternity. As if this is all there is to life. Come on, what do you think dreams are for when we sleep? They are harbingers of the realities far beyond the shores of planet earth –waiting to embrace us when we step over the threshold.

Then it is time I posed the question, are you living or dead? Because in all your choice making, if you have not made the greatest choice – if you have not chosen Jesus Christ, then all your choices would count for dung. Come on, dead men do not make choices that amount to life. The dead cannot bring forth life. Only life begets life. God can only sustain a personal relationship with those that have chosen to accept the life of His Son Jesus Christ. Hence He is the God of the living only. The dead only whisper and grope in pavilions of eternal restlessness. This ought not to be so. As long as you breathe, as long as you can still make choices, God's everlasting arms are stretched wide open to tuck you into His eternal rest.

Time is a gift. Your wise use of it will determine the outcome of your life here and here after. It is a privilege to belong to the land of the living. All the choices one needs to make can only be made in time. Time itself is a portal of opportunity God has given every living soul to choose wisely. This portal shall not remain open forever. In the fullness of all things, time's portal shall be closed. Of course before the coming of the great day of the Lord, this portal shall be closed over individual lives. Anyone that vacates the land of the living has had the portal of time over them closed. After time, no more choice making, only consequences of eternal proportions!

So, I, by the mercies of God implore you to join the living family of God today. It is so simple yet most solemn. If you do not have a personal relationship with God, if you do not have the life of the son of the living God, Jesus Christ, you can make a choice right now. Or, if you once had a vibrant relationship with God and do not anymore due to reasons best known to you, it is not late, there is plenty of room in Jesus Christ for repentance and rededication. Let your heart reach out as you open up to receive the living God into your heart. The eternal rest of your soul is the greatest choice you can make for yourself. Do what you can;

choose while you can, to ensure your soul is secured in the Ark of God's salvation.

You can pray to Him and ask Him sincerely into your heart this moment. Believe and mean every word you say, ask him to forgive your sins and empower you to live for Him. Ask Him to shine His light upon your heart, your feet and your path so you can be rejuvenated into experiencing the privileges accruable to the family of His beloved Son, Jesus Christ! You can reach out to a Bible-believing church, reach out to a cluster of other believers nearest to you or contact our ministry through any of our social media platforms for help on any questions you might have. You are blessed in Jesus Name. Amen!

CHAPTER TEN

YOUR CHOICE DETERMINES YOUR VOICE

Now there were four leprous men at the entrance of the gate; and they said to one another, "Why are we sitting here until we die? If we say, 'We will enter the city,' the famine is in the city, and we shall die there. And if we sit here, we die also. Now therefore, come, let us surrender to the army of the Syrians. If they keep us alive, we shall LIVE; and if they kill us, we shall only DIE." And they rose at twilight to go to the camp of the Syrians; and when they had come to the outskirts of the Syrian camp, to their surprise no one was there. For the Lord had caused the army of the Syrians to hear the noise of chariots and the noise of horses – the noise of a great army; so they said to one another, "Look, the king of Israel has hired against us the kings of the Hittites and the kings of the Egyptians to attack us!"

—2 Kings 7:3-7, NKJV

This portion of Scripture is one of my favourites. I have been blessed and inspired to rise up in the grace of our Lord Jesus Christ as many times as I have read it. And, I, here feel greatly compelled by the Holy Spirit to close this book with it.

The first thing that arrests my attention is that the people involved are four lepers. I would like to assume that you know what it means to be a leper in Israel in those days. And if you do not, then here is a brief: Lepers were considered unclean and unfit to coexist and mingle with the rest of the community. This was for both religious and health reasons. Leprosy was incurable in those days and anyone who had the misfortune of having it was ruthlessly ostracised. So they were usually treated as half humans and outcasts.

Their abode in the land was always in the outskirts of the city so that contact with 'clean' people was reduced to the barest minimum. In contemporary times, you might say these people are at the bottom of society - derelicts, underprivileged, ground crawlers, bottom feeders, destitute, poorest of the poor, broken hearted, vagrants, helpless, handicaps, crumb gleaners, impossible cases, illiterates, terminally ill, beggars and wretched of the earth. They were complete write-offs and considered to be victims of fortune's frown. They of course did not possess any material thing of value. They were simply untouchable in the most negative sense of the word.

However, these zeros realized they might not have any material thing of value but they sure possessed something precious and freely given to them by God – the power to choose. And upon this realization, they decided to exercise this God-given power. After all, they were at rock bottom, surpassed in gloom only by death itself. And note that they were so low that death did not even scare them anymore. For the grave was only a few cubits away from their inglorious estate. There were two options before them:

1. To sit still in the eerie outskirts of the city and die as grotesque beasts of misfortune.

2. To move into the city and die by the sword of famine or by the hands of the Syrians.

You see, the expression *between the devil and the deep blue sea* does not quite capture the gravity of their dilemma. The odds were punctiliously stacked against them from every conceivable angle. Well, they thought it much wiser and blessed to at least die with honour. Based on the twisted nature of things, the options were a lose-lose for them. Only that one bore honour and the other did not. Verily, they did not have any material thing of worth but they had a choice. This confirms an earlier assertion I made that it does not matter how precarious and hopeless a situation is, there is always a choice to make.

Four lepers – four half humans, or so they were looked upon by the society they called their own, two unfavourable options, and one choice to make. You might argue that what they exhibited was more of courage than choice. But again I put it to you that courage is a choice just like every other virtue or vice is a choice. Choice is the engine that propels all actions and inactions, good or bad.

The four lepers again did not even know that what was actually before them was life and death. They thought it was death and death: that was indeed how bad their situation was. But somehow they felt it was better for their end to come in honour rather than be without it. So they decided to conquer indecision, apathy, vile delusion, passivity and wishful thinking and take the most practical and dangerous steps of their so-called miserable lives. If anything they decided to fall forward. This singular choice made in the cauldrons of despair caused a reverberating stir in the heavens. They seemed to be between hell and death, but their choice made all the difference and caused the wheels of salvation to begin to turn to their favour in the heavens.

Four lepers marched into what seemed to be their doom.Little did they know that the great God of heaven had decided to honour their choice by activating some physics-defying laws endemic to heaven and manifesting on earth for the first time. There is no law under heaven that can explain how the weak, staggering footsteps of four lepers could be amplified into the sonic boom from the stomping boots of a valiant army in procession. In short, an army of armed men discipline themselves to match in unison. Normally other things like chants, striking of sword and spear to shield and blowing of trumpets and wild exercise of the vocal cords are used to thicken the mystique and herald of an advancing army. But that the footsteps of four lepers – outcasts and zeros became the sound of many is what makes the story a little more interesting.

By the time the four lepers got to their supposed end, it actually turned out to be the dawn of a new beginning. There was not a single soul left in the camp of the Syrians. For they had fled in various directions for their lives. The Syrians thought they heard the deadly sound of not just the army of Israel alone, but a coalition of armies hired by the king of Israel to erase their memory from earth forever. Hallelujah! The lepers' choice proved to be the right one.

Their choice gave them a voice no man or power on earth could have given them. That is why I would like to say at this point that if you and I can only exercise our God-given power of choice in every situation we find ourselves to His glory, there is no mountain or bump that cannot be torn to pieces for our sakes. The lepers' story proves one thing: with the right exercise of the power of choice the wretched of the earth can rise to the highest heavens. The lepers chose right and lived. This means the difference between life and death is choice.

I speak to you right now by the authority vested in me by the great God of heaven, choose well and all shall be well. If you choose to do God's will always, He will always rework the odd to work for your good, because He Himself is good.

Are you considered a leper today by virtue of the multidimensional challenges in your life? Rejoice for you can make a choice today. No matter how helpless and hopeless you think you are because of the crazy nature of your situation, heaven waits on you to make the right choice so that God can intervene. Are you treated like an outcast by friends and strangers alike because of a problem threatening to collapse your universe? Rise up, embrace Christ and enjoy His abundant grace today. It is no time to brook indecision. Arise in prayer, faith, patience and hope and lay hold of the salvation of the Lord for yourself, your family, your community and nation. Rise up and make a choice if you really want to make a difference and have your vice heard.

Despair is the chain the devil uses to keep you trapped in his lair. He tells you God cannot deliver you through auto-suggestive thoughts, the words of people who yield to him and through overwhelming circumstances. He amplifies your issues and tries to belittle the abundant help you can find in Christ. He tells you that you cannot be free from that destructive habit just because it has been a part of your life for more than ten, twenty or thirty years. And goes ahead to try to make you choose to live with it instead of confronting it by opening yourself up to God's grace. He tells you your God-given dreams cannot come true because failure is hereditary in your family tree. He tells you that disease cannot be healed because it has been passed down through eight generations. But these are all lies and there is one truth: Christ. Christ is the solution to all of life's problems and questions. Wallowing in the pool of depression as powered by the devil's lies and living in the victory that is abundant in Christ requires you tomake a choice today. In Christ, the chain of despair is a myth.

It is only in Christ our potentials – our voice – can be amplified to reach the whole world with our souls intact. Only God empowers and prospers the soul at the same time. The devil is incapable of doing the same. That is why those that make a deal with the devil end up losing their soul.

All those who choose Christ end up with life. All those who chose the devil end up with death. The devil is a master in tearing the soul apart and nibbling at it in exchange for the bounties on his table until the soul is no more. Jezebel served the devil, gained power and ended up as food for dogs. Judas chose to betray Jesus and ended up as the son of perdition whose corpse hung on a rope.

Jesus Christ is a life giver, healer and multiplier. Whoever chooses Him is in for an eternity of bounties. Five loaves of bread and two fish in the hands of Jesus were multiplied to feed over five thousand souls with twelve baskets of left over. The footsteps of four lepers in the hands of God were multiplied to an armydefeating force. Choose you this day whom you will serve dear brother and sister. But as for me and my house, Christ is our Lord.

You have choice – it is humanity's most important power. So, use it well so that all will be well with your soul and the souls of all those who have been destined by God to be influenced by you, in this life and in the hereafter.

May the Great One of Zion, Supreme Architect and Builder of heaven and earth, the Great Author and Director of destiny, guide you as you navigate the world's murky waters. May your days be filled with illumination that can only be found on the face of Jesus. May your heart be filled with the burning knowledge and desire to execute His will daily. May His word be light to your feet and light to your path, and His Spirit hold your soul and mind steady as you make the right choices in the face of the most violent contradictions in Jesus' name!

OTHER BOOKS BY
AROME OSAYI